W9-AKD-959
M01

SandCastle 1

Zoo Animals

Dolphins

Carey Molter

ABDO
Publishing Company

EAU CLAIRE DISTRICT LIBRARY

T 123502

Published by SandCastle™, an imprint of ABDO Publishing Company, 4940 Viking Drive, Edina, Minnesota 55435.

Copyright © 2001 by Abdo Consulting Group, Inc. International copyrights reserved in all countries. No part of this book may be reproduced in any form without written permission from the publisher. SandCastle™ is a trademark and logo of Abdo Publishing Company.

Printed in the United States.

Cover and interior photo credits: Corbis Images, Corel, Eyewire Images.

Library of Congress Cataloging-in-Publication Data

Molter, Carey, 1973-
Dolphins / Carey Molter.
p. cm. -- (Zoo animals)
ISBN 1-57765-559-1
1. Dolphins--Juvenile literature. [1. Dolphins.] I. Title.

QL737.C432 M64 2001
599.53--dc21

2001022006

The SandCastle concept, content, and reading method have been reviewed and approved by a national advisory board including literacy specialists, librarians, elementary school teachers, early childhood education professionals, and parents.

Let Us Know

After reading the book, SandCastle would like you to tell us your stories about reading. What is your favorite page? Was there something hard that you needed help with? Share the ups and downs of learning to read. We want to hear from you! To get posted on the Abdo Publishing Company Web site, send us email at:

sandcastle@abdopub.com

About SandCastle™

Nonfiction books for the beginning reader

- Basic concepts of phonics are incorporated with integrated language methods of reading instruction. Most words are short, and phrases, letter sounds, and word sounds are repeated.
- Readability is determined by the number of words in each sentence, the number of characters in each word, and word lists based on curriculum frameworks.
- Full-color photography reinforces word meanings and concepts.
- "Words I Can Read" list at the end of each book teaches basic elements of grammar, helps the reader recognize the words in the text, and builds vocabulary.
- Reading levels are indicated by the number of flags on the castle.

Look for more SandCastle books in these three reading levels:

Level 1
(one flag)

Grades Pre-K to K
5 or fewer words per page

Level 2
(two flags)

Grades K to 1
5 to 10 words per page

Level 3
(three flags)

Grades 1 to 2
10 to 15 words per page

Many dolphins live in oceans.

Some dolphins live in zoos.

This dolphin eats fish.

These dolphins swim fast.

Dolphins can jump very high.

EAU CLAIRE DISTRICT LIBRARY

All dolphins have fins.

A dolphin has many teeth.

This dolphin squeaks.

Have you seen a dolphin?

Words I Can Read

Nouns

A noun is a person, place, or thing

dolphin (DOL-fin) pp. 9, 17, 19, 21
dolphins (DOL-finz) pp. 5, 7, 11, 13, 15
fins (FINZ) p. 15
fish (FISH) p. 9
oceans (OH-shuhnz) p. 5
teeth (TEETH) p. 17
zoos (ZOOZ) p. 7

Verbs

A verb is an action or being word

can (KAN) p. 13
eats (EETSS) p. 9
has (HAZ) p. 17
have (HAV) pp. 15, 21
jump (JUHMP) p. 13
live (LIV) pp. 5, 7
seen (SEEN) p. 21
squeaks (SKWEEKSS) p. 19
swim (SWIM) p. 11

More About Dolphins
Match the Words to the Pictures

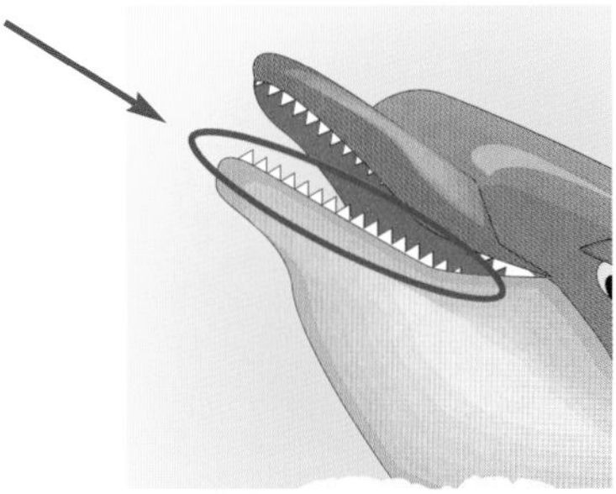

fin

fish

teeth

jump

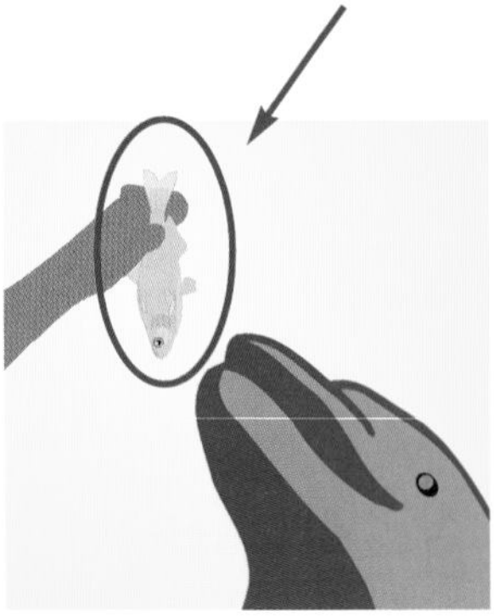

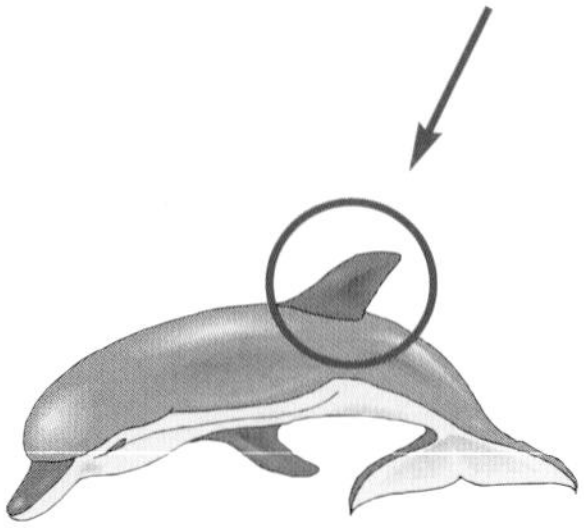

EAU CLAIRE DISTRICT LIBRARY